UPCITY SERVICE(S)

Dominic Taylor

I0139972

BROADWAY PLAY PUBLISHING INC
224 E 62nd St, NY, NY 10065
www.broadwayplaypub.com
info@broadwayplaypub.com

UPCITY SERVICE(S)
© Copyright 2005 by Dominic Taylor

.

First printing: July 2005
I S B N: 0-88145-265-3

Book design: Marie Donovan
Word processing: Microsoft Word
Typographic controls: Xerox Ventura Publisher 2.0 P E
Typeface: Palatino
Printed and bound in the U S A

CHARACTERS & SETTING

JACQUEEDA, *black woman, twenties*
POPPY, *black man, thirties*
SISTER BERRING, *African-American woman*
CANUTE FORBES, *West-Indian Man*

Eight T Vs

147th Street and Broadway in Manhattan. The street is a one-way traveling west. The north side of the street. From left to right there is a 3' x 4' imitation Persian rug, a streetlight, a fire plug/hydrant, and a burgundy 1987 Lincoln Continental.

There is a liquor store on the corner that has the roll gates down. Above the liquor store are eight windows. Each window contains a television that we do not see. At appropriate times, the T Vs will glow and sing.

STRUCTURE

Section 1—Devotional
Section 2—Scripture
Section 3—Sermon
Section 4—Benediction

TIME

Year 2003

Section 1—Dawn
Section 2—9:00 A M
Section 3—11:00 A M
Section 4—1:00 P M

Plays are not representational, they are presentational.

for Wislyn, Barbara and Keli

special thanks from the Publisher to Mac Wellman for his support of this and many other important American playwrights.

DEVOTIONAL

(At Rise: The streetlight turns off as the dawn breaks.)

*(*JACQUEEDA *enters. She is walking south down Broadway. She looks both ways on 147th Street. She begins to walk east.)*

*(*SISTER BERRING *enters walking west down 147th. She is dressed in a conservative manner. She has on a skirt and shoes that are sensible. She has a brick in each hand. She seems to be cheerful, almost humming.)*

JACQUEEDA: Sister. Hey sister.

SISTER BERRING: Good morning.

JACQUEEDA: You seen Poppy?

SISTER BERRING: Not this morning.

JACQUEEDA: You seen him last night?

SISTER BERRING: Oh no. I saw him yesterday, but not in the evening. I try not to spend too much time in the...

JACQUEEDA: You aint seen him yet?

SISTER BERRING: Not today.

JACQUEEDA: Damn!

(Beat)

SISTER BERRING: *(With sincerity)* Jacqueeda, what would you do if you died tonight?

JACQUEEDA: Now don't ask me no bullshit. And don't be handing me no tract.

SISTER BERRING: I'd never do that. It was just a question.

JACQUEEDA: You ain't seen him?

SISTER BERRING: No.

JACQUEEDA: All right.

(SISTER BERRING *exits. She walks west off stage.*)

(JACQUEEDA *paces.*)

(CANUTE *enters the space walking down Broadway. He has a broom, and a dustpan on a stick.*)

(*He sweeps up in front of the liquor store.*)

(*He begins by the rug.*)

JACQUEEDA: Hey Mister C.

CANUTE: Good morning.

JACQUEEDA: You seen Poppy?

CANUTE: Have I seen the man? Of course, I have seen the man, that's how I know his identity. I know his name and his face....

JACQUEEDA: Today.

CANUTE: This morning, I have not seen him. He is not a man who does much in the morning.

JACQUEEDA: I got to ask him something.

CANUTE: Well why not go to the man's house?

JACQUEEDA: I can't do that. It's too early.

CANUTE: But it's not too early for you to be on the corner, asking a man, working a job, for another man. A man, that I must indicate, I am not in charge of...

JACQUEEDA: O K Mister C.

CANUTE: Ask me If I seen the man, no good morning, but have I seen the man...

JACQUEEDA: I know.

(Continues sweeping.)

CANUTE: People in this country, always looking for something. When I first got here, that is what I recall.

(As he continues, she looks down the street, but eventually fades north, up Broadway.)

CANUTE: I come in this country; man asks me what have I seen. The question asked as if my vision—my looking at things is different than his. Your vision is nothing more than your eyes. The cameras of the soul. Now the perception of what I have seen, here or at home, that is made from another thing entirely.

Muhammad places his rug here, and he asks me— he does not demand—because you cannot make a man work with you, when you demand. He asks me to take care of his rug. Sweep around it; roll it up, if it is to rain. Some people look at that and say, why would the man lay down a hundred and twenty-five rugs all over Manhattan for his prayers? I tell people, they are his rugs, his prayers. It does not hurt the concrete, it does not bother me. The man has no problem with me. He drives his cab; he stops when he here or it's time and him pray.

He don't ask me to pray. He don't want you to join him. That does not bother me. So it could stay here. Now if meat make your brother stumble, eat no meat. What me see in this country is many people are carnivores, do you understand?

(He stops for a moment. He looks for Jacqueeda. She is gone.)

CANUTE: Ask me if I seen the man?

(SISTER BERRING walks east across the stage.)

(She does not have any bricks in her hands.)

SISTER BERRING: Good morning.

CANUTE: Good morning, sister.

(She continues off.)

CANUTE: Civility is the most difficult thing to find in a jungle of concrete.

(He continues to sweep. He sweeps by the Lincoln. POPPY enters, traveling down Broadway and then looks east down 147th street.)

POPPY: You seen Jacqueeda?

CANUTE: When you are in the crows' nest on a ship, what do you call that position?

POPPY: I ain't on Jeopardy.

CANUTE: I don't know what you're on.

POPPY: The television show.

CANUTE: I don't have a television.

POPPY: I didn't ask you if you had a television, it's a television program.

CANUTE: One way you can tell if people are poor.

POPPY: Look...

CANUTE: When you walk into someone's house— who is poor—the first thing you see in there is a T V. You notice that?

POPPY: Look man...

CANUTE: Because you have never been in anyone's home who was wealthy.

POPPY: You aint seen her?

CANUTE: She was just here looking for you.

POPPY: Where did she go?

CANUTE: I saw her, but she did not indicate to me— not that she need to—where she was going?

POPPY: You make things difficult.

CANUTE: I came here to do a job, and I'm doing my job I did not make it more complicated. Why did you come here?

POPPY: I ain't gonna say nothing else to you. Can't get no straight answers from you West Indians.

CANUTE: I did not know that my job was to answer to you.

POPPY: I'ma leave you alone.

CANUTE: You ain't going to leave me nothing for I must leave you.

(CANUTE *exits.* POPPY *looks left then right.*)

(POPPY *looks at the Lincoln; then he looks inside.*)

(SISTER BERRING *enters walking west with a brick in each hand.*)

POPPY: You seen Jacqueeda?

SISTER BERRING: When I saw her last she was standing right where you are now.

POPPY: Where she go?

SISTER BERRING: She didn't tell me. She was looking for you.

POPPY: Damn!

SISTER BERRING: Poppy?

POPPY: Yeah.

SISTER BERRING: What would you do if you died tonight?

POPPY: What would I do? I'd be dead. I wouldn't be doing nothing.

SISTER BERRING: Where would you go?

POPPY: Wilson's funeral home.

SISTER BERRING: They're out of business, but...

POPPY: I aint got no time to be about...shit.

SISTER BERRING: O K. *(She begins to exit west.)*

POPPY: You seen the Deacon.

SISTER BERRING: Who?

POPPY: Deacon Derricott.

SISTER BERRING: Today?

POPPY: Yes, today. I don't care if he was at your house yesterday.

SISTER BERRING: No.

POPPY: *(To himself)* When did he park his car here?

SISTER BERRING: I don't know.

POPPY: I wasn't asking you.

(She starts to leave.)

SISTER BERRING: Have a nice day.

POPPY: Why you gonna tell me to do the impossible?

SISTER BERRING: I was hoping. I wasn't telling you nothing. I was hoping. *(She exits.)*

(He looks back at the car. He walks to the corner, looks north and then south. He walks east exits off.)

(As he exits, the televisions in the eight windows above the liquor store turn on. Each window will have an identical television, although all we may see is the blue light. When the window has a part the blue light should grow brighter. Some shades are down slightly.)

(The windows are indicated by numbers.)

ONE: *I've*

TWO: *Got*

THREE: *One*

FOUR: *Question*

FIVE: *For*

SIX: *God*

ONE: *I've*

TWO: *Got*

THREE: *One*

FOUR: *Question*

FIVE: *For*

SIX: *God*

SEVEN: *Do you have section eight in heaven?*

EIGHT: *I've heard talk of the mansions,*
and I assume that those are for the righteous.
But do you have a place God, for the wrong of us.

SEVEN: *I' ve got family and friends, who have done wrong for*
so long,
That doing right might kill them.

EIGHT: *I know they've got no mansion coming their way,*
And hell is a pretty steep price to pay

SEVEN: *These people aren't that bad,*
They just don't seem to think

EIGHT: *They were born poor so the change won't phase them*

SEVEN: *Eternity in the projects will be a thing that they are*
familiar with.

EIGHT: *As opposed to the fiery pit.*
So God you see what I mean.

TWO, THREE, FOUR, FIVE, SIX:
I've got one question for God.

I've got one question for God.
I've got one question for God.

SEVEN: *Do you have any projects?*

EIGHT: *See god it may seem obvious to you, and you must have a master plan, but I wonder all the time.*

SEVEN: *What is the fate of my uncle, my father, my cousin, my sister, my brother, my niece.*

EIGHT: *They have not been as good as me.*

SEVEN: *They don't deserve my rewards, so I wonder what you will do, with the sinner that's not so sinful and the saint that's not so saintly And purgatory seems to be a place for no one.*

ONE: *So.*

TWO, THREE, FOUR, FIVE, SIX:
I've got one question for God.
(Loud clap. Gospel Choir Black Baptist church clap.
If you don't know, you do need to ask someone.)
I've
(Clap)
I've got.
(Clap)
I've got one.
(Clap)

ONE: *Not two but.*

TWO, THREE, FOUR, FIVE, SIX: *One.*
(Clap)
Question
(Clap)
Question
(Clap)
Question for
(Clap)
Question for

ONE: *Who? (Clap)*

TWO, THREE, FOUR, FIVE, SIX: *God
(Clap. Clap)
I've got.*

(Clap)

ONE: *Who's got?*

(Clap)

TWO, THREE, FOUR, FIVE, SIX: *I've got.*

(Clap)

ONE: *How many?*

TWO, THREE, FOUR, FIVE, SIX: *One.*

ONE: *How many?*

TWO, THREE, FOUR, FIVE, SIX: *One*

ONE: *What?*

TWO, THREE, FOUR, FIVE, SIX: *I've got one.*

ONE: *What you got?*

TWO, THREE, FOUR, FIVE, SIX: *Question.*

ONE: *Say it again.*

TWO, THREE, FOUR, FIVE, SIX: *Question.*

ONE: *What is it?*

TWO, THREE, FOUR, FIVE, SIX: *Question for.*

ONE: *Whose question is it?*

TWO, THREE, FOUR, FIVE, SIX: *God!!!*

ONE: *What's the question?*

TWO, THREE, FOUR, FIVE, SIX: *Does heaven.*

ONE: *Not earth, but*

TWO, THREE, FOUR, FIVE, SIX: *Does heaven.*

ONE: *Have what?*

TWO, THREE, FOUR, FIVE, SIX: *A Ghetto.*

(As the song ends, the T V dims, the daylight becomes brighter.)

(JACQUEEDA walks down Broadway, and turns the corner.)

(POPPY walking west.)

POPPY & JACQUEEDA: I was looking for you.

POPPY: JACQUEEDA:
I need you to do something   You got four sixty?
for me.

(End of Devotional)

SCRIPTURE

POPPY: JACQUEEDA:
Where you been?   What's happening?

POPPY: What you doing today?

JACQUEEDA: You got any money?

POPPY: That's why I want to know what your day is...

JACQUEEDA: You got four sixty?

POPPY: What you need four dollars for?

JACQUEEDA: Four dollars and sixty cents.

POPPY: You can get that.

(Beat. She has her hand out.)

POPPY: You need it now?

JACQUEEDA: Yeah.

POPPY: Look, if you got some time today, you can come off with some mad change.

JACQUEEDA: How much?

POPPY: Five or six million.

(She stares at him.)

JACQUEEDA: Today?

POPPY: Yeah today.

JACQUEEDA: Can I do it later?

POPPY: You can't do it now?

JACQUEEDA: I've got something to do right now.
That's why I need the four sixty.

POPPY: You can't chill for a minute?

JACQUEEDA: I gotta make three quick runs.

POPPY: Four sixty?

JACQUEEDA: I need to get downtown first.

POPPY: What you gotta do?

JACQUEEDA: I told you I gotta make a couple of runs.

POPPY: You can't let me know, but you want my dinero?

JACQUEEDA: You probably aint got it.

POPPY: I'm gonna let you in. I ain't taking nobody else
in. *(He sits on the Lincoln.)* One million. You can't tell
me the couple of stops you gonna make more than that.
(Beat) I might wanna run with you....

JACQUEEDA: You can't do that.

POPPY: Why you playing like you are wired for sound?
Can't tell me nothing? You and me we run like 1010
News. All the news all the time. Can't come tight on me.

JACQUEEDA: I just found out.

POPPY: Who's the father?

JACQUEEDA: Shut the fuck up.

POPPY: So what's up then?

JACQUEEDA: My father died.

POPPY: Your pops?

JACQUEEDA: They're burying him today.

POPPY: I didn't know you had a father.

JACQUEEDA: He broke the fuck out. I mean...he stayed
through high school.

POPPY: I thought that was your mother's man?

JACQUEEDA: He was the only father I ever knew.

POPPY: I thought you said he wasn't shit.

JACQUEEDA: He wasn't, but they're putting him in the ground this morning.

POPPY: I thought you had a job?

JACQUEEDA: They hold the first check.

POPPY: You get a check every two weeks, and they hold the first one? Oh, that is suspect. *(Gets off the Lincoln)*

JACQUEEDA: Keep you from quitting.

(POPPY looks up and down the street.)

JACQUEEDA: You ain't got it?

POPPY: I ain't know you played all Hallmark like that. Being sentimental and what not.

JACQUEEDA: You quit your job?

POPPY: That job wasn't shit. I can get another one. Moving boxes ain't nothing but showing up and lifting.

JACQUEEDA: Damn man.

POPPY: If you can chill, I'm telling you...I'll get you a million.

JACQUEEDA: I need four sixty.

POPPY: I gotta dollar.

JACQUEEDA: Damn it.

POPPY: Check it. Whose car is this?

JACQUEEDA: What the fuck are you talking about?

POPPY: Whose car?

(She walks to the car and looks in the window.)

JACQUEEDA: They got some change in the ashtray?

POPPY: It's Deacon Derricott's car.

(Beat)

JACQUEEDA: So?

POPPY: You ain't heard.

JACQUEEDA: Heard what?

POPPY: If I had a paper, I'd show you.

(As this comes out of his mouth, CANUTE *walks on with a vest and some newspapers.)*

CANUTE: *The News* or *The Post?*

POPPY: Post.

CANUTE: One or two?

POPPY: One.

JACQUEEDA: Why not get the News?

POPPY: Same news, but I save ten cents.

*(*CANUTE *waits while* POPPY *fishes for change to make up a quarter.)*

*(*CANUTE *looks to* JACQUEEDA.*)*

(As POPPY *counts out his pennies.)*

JACQUEEDA: How's everything, fine?

CANUTE: No. Everything is not fine. It is so and so.

JACQUEEDA: Working...

CANUTE: Working is all I do. It is not fine. I work, I turn around, I work, I turn around, I work, I turn around. Three hundred and sixty degrees, the only thing I have is work. It is not fine. Me turn around, turn around. Turn around twenty-four hours in a day. Me work eight hours one. Eight hours another. Eight hours the third. My sleep I only assume. It is not fine. It is only so and so.

(POPPY *discovers his dollar.* CANUTE *hands him some change.*)

JACQUEEDA: *(To* CANUTE*)* You got three eighty-five?

(CANUTE *looks at her and sucks his teeth.*)

CANUTE: *Post* or *Daily News?*

(POPPY *has folded out the pages and looks at them.*)

(CANUTE *walks away.*)

(*Points emphatically.* JACQUEEDA *reads.*)

JACQUEEDA: *(Reading)* God wins the lottery. Deacon Derricott a member of First Calvary Temple Church in Harlem. *(Stops reading)* This ain't Harlem.

(POPPY *points again. She continues.*)

JACQUEEDA: Is the proud holder of the only winning lottery ticket of the fifty million dollar lottery on Saturday. He has promised that all of the money will go to the Lord. *(Stops reading again)* So?

POPPY: Whose car is that?

JACQUEEDA: What does that have to do with me?

POPPY: *(Indicates the paper.)* That proves it.

JACQUEEDA: Proves what? I gotta go. Is Ron out there swiping people for a dollar?

POPPY: You talk good.

JACQUEEDA: I talk like I talk.

POPPY: No. Listen you got that job doing phone surveys.

JACQUEEDA: I ain't got no time for...

POPPY: Hold up. You talk that talk. You lay down a church line for our church...and...and he is gonna give *you* some money.

JACQUEEDA: Five million dollars?

POPPY: If you ask him right.

JACQUEEDA: Give me your seventy-five cents, and let me get the rest of my money.

POPPY: This is gonna work.

JACQUEEDA: I can't tell you how off the charts this is. That plan is totally blitzed.

(SISTER BERRING *walks across with nothing in her hands.*)

JACQUEEDA: You have any money?

SISTER BERRING: Money?

JACQUEEDA: Any cheddar, you got some coin or not?

SISTER BERRING: Not.

JACQUEEDA: Not.

SISTER BERRING: I got a question.

POPPY: Ain't nobody dying today?

SISTER BERRING: That ain't my question.

POPPY: Don't ask nothing crazy?

SISTER BERRING: If there is a God, was he sleeping during the Holocaust?

JACQUEEDA: The holocaust? God wasn't napping. How many Gods are there...

POPPY: Ain't but one God, but that ain't the holocaust. They lost, and it was because of belief, but they lost six million people. The holocaust. We lost two hundred and fifty million people on that water slave trip. Two hundred and fifty million. If that was a holocaust then what was ours? The super sized holocaust.

JACQUEEDA: But that wasn't a holocaust, in that sense, that was about the game. You know it was all about money.

POPPY: So you saying it wasn't a holocaust because the cause was money?

SISTER BERRING: Which one was about the money?

JACQUEEDA: The Jewish holocaust case, people tried to exterminate them people. Slavery was about pimping to a mad level.

POPPY: They both off the hook, but you can't talk about one, and act like the bigger numbers wasn't bigger. These fucked up folks was working out cause of money more than religion. Now God and religion ain't had nothing to do with nothing. See money was the thing.

SISTER BERRING: Which holocaust you talking about?

JACQUEEDA: Both.

(Beat)

POPPY: Why you putting God up in that shit anyway?

JACQUEEDA: Poppy is right.

SISTER BERRING: If there is a God, God doesn't start and end it all?

JACQUEEDA: You ain't got four dollars?

SISTER BERRING: No.

JACQUEEDA: God don't fuck around with cash at all.

SISTER BERRING: You don't know?

POPPY: Why are you fucking with us any way?

(SISTER BERRING walks east and off.)

JACQUEEDA: Gimme that. *(She attacks the newspaper. She flips through it front to back, then back to front. When she is at the front, she looks through the table of contents and searches for obituaries.)* Damn it. God damn it.

POPPY: What?

JACQUEEDA: Mother fucker dies and they can't give the poor nigga an obit?

POPPY: You just can't get one. You gotta pay for it.

JACQUEEDA: That ain't the case.

POPPY: That is. Don't fuck up the paper.

JACQUEEDA: Rich people die. Princess Di dies and she all over this mother...

POPPY: What is the deal with you and him, you working out some guilt?

JACQUEEDA: He lived. He lived and he can't get a line in the paper that says that.

POPPY: No sister...

JACQUEEDA: He really wasn't shit, but he did two things. Most motherfuckers don't do one, but he did two. He can't get a line?

POPPY: What he do?

JACQUEEDA: He taught me how to bet?

POPPY: Any body can bet?

JACQUEEDA: Naw. He taught me how to win?

POPPY: He didn't lose?

JACQUEEDA: Never.

POPPY: Then why you sitting here looking for four dollars?

JACQUEEDA: Cause I ain't go to the track yet? *(Beat)* For real, he couldn't lose. He didn't go to the track much. He thought it was cruel to the horses, but when he was there he wouldn't lose.

POPPY: Humanitarian motherfucker huh?

JACQUEEDA: I ain't say all of that.

POPPY: But he taught you that huh?

JACQUEEDA: Look you can't give your kids everything; you give em what you can. That's what he gave me.

POPPY: So you on your way to the track?

JACQUEEDA: I gotta go pay my respects first, then to the track. I need to get him a head stone.

POPPY: Is it a head stone or a tombstone?

JACQUEEDA: I don't know, but the store is closing today.

POPPY: The store on one forty fifth is closed.

JACQUEEDA: It's closing today. It's filling all orders, but you have to get them in today.

POPPY: Look you get my money; you can go downtown and get a stone.

JACQUEEDA: I ain't messing with your plan man. I know what I'm doing. I ain't begging on somebody else's ticket.

POPPY: Look the money is there.

JACQUEEDA: No it's not. It ain't yours and what if he says no? What you gonna do, bust him in the head?

POPPY: I don't bust nobody in the head. If I need to, I get somebody else to do it.

JACQUEEDA: (*Looking where* SISTER BERRING *exited.*) She ain't got no job?

POPPY: I don't know.

JACQUEEDA: She gotta have a job. She eats.

POPPY: She don't eat good.

JACQUEEDA: You don't know that.

POPPY: I know this; she walks with bricks from one spot to another.

JACQUEEDA: She carries the bricks, so?

POPPY: That's what she does. She don't make no money.

JACQUEEDA: She just stacks them from one spot to another.

POPPY: I guess.

JACQUEEDA: But nobody pays her?

POPPY: I don't think so.

JACQUEEDA: How she eat?

POPPY: She aint got four dollars.

JACQUEEDA: You know that?

POPPY: Yeah I do. People give her stuff. Clothes, food, but don't nobody pay her. *(Beat)* You need to work on your pitch.

JACQUEEDA: My pitch?

POPPY: For the deacon.

JACQUEEDA: He ain't coming off with no money.

POPPY: *(Opening the paper)* He got fifty million dollars, you can't talk him outta no money? You ain't got enough rap to get nothin from somebody who got fifty million? He like women too, come on.

JACQUEEDA: Oh he'd come off with something.

POPPY: How you so sure?

JACQUEEDA: I got this job now, reading the screen, rapping to folks I don't see.

POPPY: How would you do it?

JACQUEEDA: Well, you know he wants to help God out so you...you gotta hit him with a God rap.

(She acts like she's picked up a phone. He acts like he is on the other end.)

JACQUEEDA: *Ah salaam a lakum.*

POPPY: Click.

JACQUEEDA: Oh that's weak.

POPPY: He's gonna run the other way. We ain't rolling no money for Muhammad. He aint on no afro-asiatic...

JACQUEEDA: All right, all right.
Ring.
(Picks up the phone)
May Yahweh,

POPPY: Click.

JACQUEEDA: I was just going to start there.

POPPY: He ain't gonna keep you on the phone. He don't know you. *(Beat)* Does he know you?

JACQUEEDA: No.

POPPY: You gotta bring the thing.

JACQUEEDA: The Christian thing?

POPPY: Them other God's may be true, but he's only gonna come off to his God.

JACQUEEDA: Well then why don't he just sign the check over to his church?

POPPY: That's where your skills come in.

JACQUEEDA: I got it.
Bring.
Brother Derricott greetings and may God be the glory.
I am Sister Smith...

POPPY: Click. Who is named Smith?

JACQUEEDA: Come one now, he ain't gonna click on a name.

POPPY: They can click on anything. You never know what it could be. Look he a Black man, give him a Black name.

JACQUEEDA: What's a Black name?

POPPY: Not Smith. Try Williams or Jones. Don't try to make up an African name, keep it simple. Try Cole or Wilson.

JACQUEEDA: Ring.

(He picks up the phone.)

JACQUEEDA: Hello and blessings brother Derricott. I am Sister Williams from the Mount Zion A M E Baptist

POPPY: Click

JACQUEEDA: What?

POPPY: You can't be A M E and Baptist.

JACQUEEDA: How you know that?

POPPY: I just know it. Trust me on that.

JACQUEEDA: You make the call.

POPPY: No baby, you the best on the phone. I couldn't flow like you flow. I ain't never keep no telephone job. You be out there working with the free knives and what not.

JACQUEEDA: When I'm in there. I be pounding some phone.

POPPY: You got some skillz.

JACQUEEDA: Mad skillz.

POPPY: Show what you got. Ring.

JACQUEEDA: Hello Brother Derricott. Glory to God, I'm Sister Williams from the Mount Zion A M E Church. We here at the church, have been in Brooklyn trying to do the Lord's will. We have a few outreach missions,

but our two main programs have been dealing with
substance abuse and sick and infirmed children.
As I know that you must know, the city has cut back
on social services. The city in the ongoing attempt to
separate Church and state, is attempting to separate
Church from doing good work. We will keep on,
Lord willing, doing good work; if the Lord gives us
the strength, mentally, spiritually, and financially to
maintain. But as you would know, anything that you
could bless us with, would allow us to continue the
Lord's work with these sick children, or these fallen
brothers and sisters. We are here to help them when
they are too weak to fight. Brother Derricott what
would be a level that you could find comfortable
giving? Brother Derricott? Brother Derricott?

POPPY: Where did you get that from?

JACQUEEDA: What?

POPPY: That was good. You just made that up?

JACQUEEDA: That's what all these donation joints are.
They end asking for your level, and then you ask for
more.

POPPY: How much do they come off with?

JACQUEEDA: Thousands. They never want to look
cheap. I never got millions but I never called someone
with fifty million.

POPPY: That you know of?

JACQUEEDA: True that. That I know of. I don't know if
any of these people passed the money. They told me
they got the checks, but I never seen any.

POPPY: They pay you though?

JACQUEEDA: Hell yeah.

POPPY: Well then they had to get the money.

JACQUEEDA: True.

POPPY: But how can we get him to pass off millions?

JACQUEEDA: Like I said, that is mad, mad money. Long dollars.

POPPY: I need that money.

JACQUEEDA: You can't work? What, you sick?

POPPY: I ain't working for nobody no more. I can't go out like that.

JACQUEEDA: So you need millions?

POPPY: That way I won't have to work no more.

JACQUEEDA: If you weren't working what would you do?

POPPY: Chill.

JACQUEEDA: All day.

POPPY: All day and all night.

JACQUEEDA: You working now.

POPPY: It don't matter. All I be doing is sweating about some coin.

JACQUEEDA: You don't want to sweat that no more?

POPPY: Not about no money shit. A million, a couple million, I would sweat no more about money.

JACQUEEDA: What would you sweat about then?

POPPY: I don't know, but it wouldn't be about money.

JACQUEEDA: I heard that.

(Beat)

POPPY: Your father taught you about the ponies?

JACQUEEDA: Something like that.

POPPY: How you do it?

JACQUEEDA: It ain't hard. *(Beat)* But it ain't easy.

POPPY: You put some voodoo on it?

JACQUEEDA: You start with the facts. If you aint got the Forum, then the paper will do. That's where you start. Stephen knew nothing about school, but he knew about the homework of nature.

POPPY: So he bet the favorites?

JACQUEEDA: No. He'd say, you bet favorites all the time, to win, at the end of the God damn day you gonna have less money than you started - a lot less. You know you can't shoot fish in a barrel. After the first shot the barrel is busted.

POPPY: So what are you supposed to look for?

JACQUEEDA: What he told me is; figure out what will happen. Not who will win. What you try to do is to find out, with certainty, what will be the most likely event to happen with the first three. You can get paid by betting on Show alone. If you get me two dollars, by the ninth race, I'll have five hundred. That way I can get Stephen a head stone.

POPPY: What do you mean?

JACQUEEDA: The store is closing today.

POPPY: I know that. How you get five hundred?

JACQUEEDA: Double your money each race. By the ninth you've got five hundred and twleve dollars.

POPPY: You won't lose.

JACQUEEDA: I won't lose. That's why I need four-sixty.

POPPY: You going to the track or to O T B?

JACQUEEDA: Gotta go to Aqueduct. Gotta see the horse.

POPPY: I hear that.

JACQUEEDA: You can believe what you want, but you gotta deal with what you see.

POPPY: No doubt.

JACQUEEDA: That's what I need the four dollars for.

(CANUTE *enters from the north heading south.*)

JACQUEEDA: Hey, Mister C, you got four dollars?

(*He has a shovel in his hand. He looks at them both.*)

JACQUEEDA: Look man if you aint got it, you aint got it. But if you working like a dog—and you are working like a dog—how come you aint got no money?

CANUTE: I'm on my way to work now.

JACQUEEDA: I'll pay you back. They're holding two checks. If they weren't holding my first check, I'd have money now.

CANUTE: Tell them to advance you.

POPPY: Don't talk to him.

CANUTE: That's right.

JACQUEEDA: I know you've got it.

CANUTE: How does my money, become your money?

JACQUEEDA: It would be a loan.

CANUTE: Never a borrower or a lender be.

JACQUEEDA: Come on man.

CANUTE: Why don't you do like all the other girls do when they need a few dollars?

(POPPY *backs up.*)

(JACQUEEDA *walks up to* CANUTE.)

JACQUEEDA: That was fucked up.

CANUTE: If you don't work in that manner, why feel insulted? If you said it to me, it would not affect me. Lie should never hurt you.

JACQUEEDA: To say that to me must mean that you think low of me.

CANUTE: Child, you shouldn't care what I think of you. You wanted some money. I told you what some people in your condition do; I meant nothing by it. If it is not a temptation, then leave it alone. You come like you wanna cuff me. Your best plan is to think of how you could get your money. Best bet, I think is working for it. Method of employment is up to you. But to come to me, a man you do not know...to come up to me...and ask me about something that has nothing to do with me, it makes no sense.

JACQUEEDA: Well don't say nothing to me then.

POPPY: Leave him alone.

CANUTE: My sentiments exactly; I have work to do. *(He walks south with his shovel.)*

POPPY: Don't pay him no mind. We'll get some money.

JACQUEEDA: I need the money man. They're going to bury him soon.

POPPY: You gotta get him an obit too.

JACQUEEDA: How much you gotta pay for an obit?

POPPY: We can find that out. Aint nobody I know had one, but I'll find out.

JACQUEEDA: He did me a solid. I should at least try to get him that.

(Beat)

POPPY: Go to my spot; I need to do set something up real quick.

JACQUEEDA: I ain't got time to be messing with the Deacon.

POPPY: If we run up on the Deacon, we'll try something, you know?

JACQUEEDA: We gonna steal the ticket?

POPPY: Everybody know he won. *(He flips the paper open.)* Just go to my spot...give me a minute

JACQUEEDA: I ain't got no time....

POPPY: You want the money or not?

JACQUEEDA: Don't be long.

POPPY: I aint...look.

(They have made a non-verbal agreement.)

(She walks east. He walks north. T Vs begin to glow again.)

SIX: *My God*

TWO: *You know*

THREE: *You know*

FOUR: *You know*

FIVE: *What I want.*

SEVEN: *Our God*

TWO: *You know*

THREE: *You know*

FOUR: *You know*

FIVE: *What I want.*

EIGHT: *When you look in my heart*

SIX: *My god.*

EIGHT: *When you see that look in my eye God.*

ONE: *You know we call you God,*

SEVEN: *Cause you've got all the juice.*

ONE: *Well that's what God means.*

SEVEN: *The big cheese in the big league and when we call you*

FOUR: *You know what we want.*

SIX: *Well my God*

THREE: *You know*

FOUR: *Only you know*

FIVE: *What I want.*

TWO: *I might not know*

FOUR: *But you know.*

THREE: *And since you are almighty*

FIVE: *And you know what I want*

TWO, THREE, FOUR: *Give it to me*

Give it to me

Give it to me

TWO, THREE, FOUR, SIX: *Right Now.*

Right Now God.

SEVEN: *Since you can see*

SIX: *Not just what I need*
But what my wants would be

SEVEN: *I believe it's your mission*

SIX: *If you are God*

ONE: *And I know you are*

SIX: *Then the way to prove it to the rest of the world*

SEVEN: *Would be if you give me everything I want.*

TWO: *Cause I'll tell all*

THREE: *If you give me all.*

TWO: *It seems like a just deal*

THREE: *And I knew you are a just one.*

FOUR, FIVE: *The world has turned its back on you, because they think you are leaving too much for us.*

SIX, SEVEN: *God*

SIX: *My god*

TWO: *You know*

THREE: *You know*

FOUR: *You know*

FIVE: *What I want.*

ONE: *Since I know you have all the juice*

SEVEN: *My god*

SIX: *My dear sweet god*

TWO, THREE, FOUR, FIVE: *Give me what I want.*

SIX: *And give it to me*

SEVEN: *Not any time in the future*

TWO, THREE, FOUR, FIVE:
But God if you want the converts that

ONE: *I know you need.*

TWO, THREE, FOUR, FIVE:
Give me what I want
Give me what I want
Come on and give me what I want
Right Now.
I need it, right now
I want it, right now
Right now.

(During the last song)

(SISTER BERRING *walks west again with two bricks. As she walks she acknowledges that the day has moved further ahead.*)

(*The lights balance back.*)

(*End of Scripture*)

SERMON

(As lights get brighter, JACQUEEDA *comes running on stage. Running west. She runs to the corner of 147th and Broadway.)*

(She screams as if the scream will make everything correct.)

JACQUEEDA: Poppy! Yo Poppy! Where you at?! You fake non-Spanish speaking Spanglish motherfucker. Where you at with my four dollars and sixty cents? God damn nigga, where the fuck you at? Running around Harlem...you running around this mother fucking spot like you a baller... you aint even a playa. Can't make four sixty come, shit. Poppy, I need that mother fucking money now man. They bury that old man, I aint never gonna find him. They don't make no maps of where they lay poor niggas. Poor niggas? Them mother fuckers but landfill. God damn Poppy! I mean, I could sell some shit off this Lincoln, but ain't nobody over here. Poppy, all the other buster motherfuckers show up after the liquor stores open. God damn.

Where's a mother fucking crack head when you need one? Poppy what the fuck you doing!? Running around looking for a deacon who aint got no time for your ass no way. Poppy, man. You ass. Motherfuckers always tell you to check your friends. Poor motherfuckers keep you poor. It aint just that the nigga poor, but he always got a mother fucking scheme. A nigga with a scheme is always a snitch away from being locked up, always. Niggas locked up; they can't do nothing. They get in and come back with more schemes. After being locked

down, they get to read two books. Then that new,
two read, motherfucker is a true pain in the ass.
K R S One...back in the day said, the library is where
all the lies are buried. That ain't the case.

God damn man! Mother fucking shit. Can't cop a four
dollars? The old man saved me from his sick brother,
when I was young and I can't spot him up with some
granite. Yo Poppy! Only thing we know is that we go.
And some mother fucking body ought to notice that
shit. Poppy the motherfucker is dead. He ain't lie to me,
and I want to do two things for his dead ass. Where the
fuck are you man? I knew you ain't find the Deacon,
cause you'd be here trying to get me to lay some shit
on him. "Hello and greetings brother Derricott." All
that shit is easy. I gotta say goodbye to that man.

Everybody else get over. Everybody. Once you got to
some levels, all you do is get over. Them motherfuckers
get Nike to sponsor their death. Those motherfuckers
feet don't touch the ground. They go out here living
like they super heroes. Then the time that somebody
say something to them, they try to take you out. Bring
you down, make you trip on what aint real. That's why
they killed him. He was working security at this joint.
Genome research joint. Everybody running around
looking for the key. The secret. He said, if you need a
remote control for the D N A you ever think that that
Watson & Crick model was wrong? That's what he says
to me and the next day he's dead. The mysteries we
believe we can't challenge should probably be looked
at. Next day he's dead. But the mysteries that are real
mysteries we can't challenge cause real mysteries don't
get solved. They mysteries.

Poppy! Man it ain't like I asked you for too much.
I ain't ask you to answer no question. I ain't ask you
to find the remote control to D N A. I ain't ask you
about no shit about life. I asked your trifling ass for four
dollars. Sixteen fucking quarters. It's some money. Any

buster could come up with four. Sell some oregano as
a nickel, but you couldn't. And I'll give it back to you
before the day is up. You chasing a deacon. Shit! On
another nigga pipe dream.
    Poppy man. *(She is about to leave but does not. She walks
to Muhammad's rug. She thinks about doing something to
the rug.)* And where the fuck has Muhammad been?
Downtown? Where the fuck he been? He probably got
five dollars. He out here driving motherfuckers around
to nowhere. Get in his car all he ever say is "five
dollars", "ten dollars", or "no I don't go there."
Like he stuck. Like he can't change shit up. And that be
your problem. Hit your ass with some flexibility. You
couldn't come like that. It's the five and ten tradition.
Tradition comes running in the face with evolution, and
he always end up with same shit. Some more conflict.
Less sleep for everyone. You included. Now if he could
run me here or there for less. Or just change up, but that
aint none of my business. I wish his ass was around for
one simple reason. I would want him to spot me five.
A quick five, cause if I jump on the train and tell the
woman in the booth... shit, brother be down there
looking for the dollar swipe. She'd be like no. Call the
M T A police...and I can't be locked trying to creep on
a train. That makes no sense. To do time for something
like that? I can't.
    Even if I got to the funeral, what would I look like
trying to get somebody to pass me three dollars? How
can you ask somebody for a loan at a funeral? Cause
aint that the last payment? You know you don't...can't
pay no more. Even though he was like a father to me;
it don't matter. When would they see me again? Ain't
nobody coming up here to look for nobody.
    Aint nothing up here no more. Not for nobody in
their right mind.
    Poppy your damn ass.
    Poppy look man. God damn. *(She walks on top of the*

hood of the Lincoln. She looks east and then the west.)
No alarm on this motherfucker? Is this the last car in
New York City without an alarm? Must not be shit in
there. Poppy where could you be? Where could I go
and look for you? And time is running out. Waiting
around for you. Time is running on me, and run out
on that old man. And when time is gone, with money
nowhere, what do I got? What can you do? In this land
of nothing, if the liquor store aint open, then aint even
no money passed in the daylight.

   What happens to the people? Who do you turn to,
when your friends is gone? When your money is gone?
Who do you turn to when friends are nowhere? Where
do you go to when there is nowhere to go? Where do
you go? *(Pause. Stomps her foot)* Now some punks go to
crime. Other punks go to some religious shit. Others
step to narcotics, but I ain't going out like none of that.
Cause the fact, the mother fucking true fact is there is
always somewhere to go. You aint got nowhere to go,
cause you ain't looked. Jacqueeda look. Jacqueeda look!

*(*SISTER BERRING *walks east again empty handed.*
JACQUEEDA *jumps down from the car.)*

JACQUEEDA: How come you ain't got four dollars?

SISTER BERRING: What do you mean?

JACQUEEDA: How come you ain't got four dollars?

SISTER BERRING: I don't need it.

JACQUEEDA: Shut the fuck up.

SISTER BERRING: O K. *(She starts to walk off.)*

JACQUEEDA: You seen Poppy?

SISTER BERRING: Not recently. You probably saw him
last.

JACQUEEDA: Shit. How long?

SISTER BERRING: I guess an hour.

JACQUEEDA: All right.

(SISTER BERRING *has almost left the stage.* JACQUEEDA *calls her back.*)

JACQUEEDA: You seen Deacon Derricott?

SISTER BERRING: No. I don't think anybody gonna see him.

JACQUEEDA: You don't think millionaires walk the streets?

SISTER BERRING: You haven't heard?

JACQUEEDA: That he hit the lotto? It was in the paper.

SISTER BERRING: No. He didn't hit it.

JACQUEEDA: What are you talking about? You know what the paper said. It had his picture too.

SISTER BERRING: No. He made a fake ticket.

JACQUEEDA: Shut the fuck up.

SISTER BERRING: He took some money from the church's building fund. He had to pay it back.

JACQUEEDA: How much he take?

SISTER BERRING: I don't know but he needed some money. He had a computer and a copy machine.

JACQUEEDA: You lying.

SISTER BERRING: Story comes to me, that he spent the last part of the money on lottery tickets. Maybe a thousand. And he prayed. He prayed that the Lord would let him hit. I guess the Lord wasn't listening. Then he said, well the church would be doing the Lord's work. It would be, you know, praising his holy name, so he should win. For God's sake, he should win.

JACQUEEDA: He made a fake ticket?

SISTER BERRING: He sure did.

JACQUEEDA: He shoulda known he'd get caught.

SISTER BERRING: He thought the Lord would protect him.

JACQUEEDA: The machine that prints the winning tickets keeps a record.

SISTER BERRING: He wasn't thinking about that.

JACQUEEDA: So he got nothing?

SISTER BERRING: He got locked up.

JACQUEEDA: God damn.

SISTER BERRING: I guess so.

JACQUEEDA: How'd you find out?

SISTER BERRING: I see the police putting somebody in a car. It was out in front of the barbershop. The car drove away. I asked the officer what happened. He knows me. He sees me around, so he tells me the truth.

JACQUEEDA: What did the deacon have to say?

SISTER BERRING: He was in the car, and it looked like he was praying.

JACQUEEDA: Mother fucker. *(She kicks the car.)*

SISTER BERRING: He won't be doing none of that for a while.

JACQUEEDA: What you say?

SISTER BERRING: See ya. *(She exits.)*

JACQUEEDA: Motherfucker lied. You lie, you'll cheat. You cheat, you'll steal. You'll steal, you'll kill. Damn it.

(POPPY enters and is very excited.)

POPPY: J come on, the Deacon's at the barbershop, getting his haircut.

JACQUEEDA: No he's not.

POPPY: You seen him?

JACQUEEDA: You ain't seen him.

POPPY: Sonny told me that he was there.

JACQUEEDA: He ain't in there no more.

POPPY: How you know?

JACQUEEDA: That nigga is locked up.

POPPY: What are you talking about?

JACQUEEDA: Brother deacon is preaching behind bars now.

POPPY: What you mean?

JACQUEEDA: He made a fake ticket.

POPPY: You lyin.

JACQUEEDA: That wasn't in the paper, huh?

POPPY: Who told you this?

JACQUEEDA: Sister with the bricks.

POPPY: What does she know?

JACQUEEDA: She saw it.

POPPY: Shut up.

JACQUEEDA: She talked to the cops.

POPPY: Nobody talks to the cops.

JACQUEEDA: She walks around with bricks in her hands. She talk to anybody.

POPPY: She saw them arrest him?

JACQUEEDA: Picked him up by the barbershop.

POPPY: Fuck.

JACQUEEDA: You aint happen up on four dollars did you?

POPPY: Who can you trust?

JACQUEEDA: Clearly not anybody with a church.

POPPY: It was the money.

JACQUEEDA: You ain't know the man anyway.

POPPY: How you know she aint lie?

JACQUEEDA: What she gotta lie for?

POPPY: You told her you were getting some money?

JACQUEEDA: Hell no. I aint never thought I was getting none. I was only looking to help you. I just wanted four dollars and sixty cents. You want the four million.

POPPY: She told you this without you asking her nothing?

JACQUEEDA: I was looking for you. I told her I was looking for you. She ain't see you, so I asked if she seen the deacon. She said yeah, in the back of a police car.

POPPY: God damn it.

JACQUEEDA: I guess you didn't get the four dollars?

POPPY: All your thinking is small.

JACQUEEDA: I'm thinking about all the money I need. I get that much, I can get the rest.

POPPY: You don't earn no money at the track.

JACQUEEDA: Ain't no way for you to get me no money?

(POPPY *sits on the Lincoln.*)

POPPY: I quit my job.

JACQUEEDA: You ain't working at all?

POPPY: Motherfuckers always trying to put you down on that shit. They act like you stupid. Treat you like you aint nobody. Treat you like you a Hebrew slave. If you get hurt, they just roll on past you. I said first time I get a break—win the lottery, get a slip and fall on the train, a settlement anything—I was going to be like fuck that job. Paying me six dollars and fifty cents a motherfucking hour. I don't even bring back two hundred a week. When I read that the Deacon won, and you had the phone job, I just put two and two together. I said yeah, I'm over now. I got to the next level that everybody is talking about. I thought I finally caught a break. Finally.

JACQUEEDA: But it wasn't your ticket no way.

POPPY: What?

JACQUEEDA: It wasn't your ticket. It was the deacon's fake ticket.

POPPY: I know.

JACQUEEDA: You should be glad cause, if it was yours, they'da locked you up too.

POPPY: But that was my break, my shot.

JACQUEEDA: To be locked up?

POPPY: It was my shot.

(SISTER BERRING *walks west with two bricks in her hands.*)

(POPPY *encroaches.*)

POPPY: Why'd you lie?

SISTER BERRING: Huh?

POPPY: They couldn't have locked up the deacon.

SISTER BERRING: City cops were there, but they put him in a federal car.

JACQUEEDA: It's a federal offense that makes sense.

POPPY: Why you taking her side?

JACQUEEDA: There ain't no sides.

POPPY: How did they find out?

SISTER BERRING: I don't know.

JACQUEEDA: The machines register every ticket printed. It wasn't hard.

POPPY: Why didn't you help him?

SISTER BERRING: I was just coming back this way....

POPPY: It's people like you. The Black man is getting locked up for something, he didn't do, and you stand by and watch.

SISTER BERRING: What was I supposed to do?

POPPY: *(He approaches her menacingly.)* Help the man! You see he needed help. If you were in trouble... *(Beat)* ...if I walked over there now and was about to bust your head open.

(SISTER BERRING is cowering.)

(CANUTE enters with his shovel.)

CANUTE: You wouldn't do that.

(Men have a moment of confrontation.)

CANUTE: Sister you all right.

SISTER BERRING: Yes. Thank you. *(To POPPY)* There was nothing I could do.

CANUTE: Gwan sister. That man made a choice. You can't clean up everyone else's mess.

SISTER BERRING: Good day. *(She exits.)*

CANUTE: Good day. What do you think you were about to do?

JACQUEEDA: That ain't none of your business.

CANUTE: Course it is. You two hanging out doing nothing. Attacking that young lady.

POPPY: You don't know what is...

CANUTE: I know exactly what is going on. You thought you had some free money coming. Now how can a man reap, if him no sow? But to your thinking...you say, well I must have sown. I must have had times harder than the next man, but that no be so. Time no hard, nor time no soft. Day but twenty-four hours. No quick, no slow. You can't look upon another man house and say, that man get less rain than you. Black, nor white, can't say that. Because man no give time, nor man no take time. Time is. Time was. Time will always be.

POPPY: What's the matter with you West Indians? Always speaking in riddle...

CANUTE: I no speak in riddle. I speak plain truth. Me speak plain, but it seem not to matter. Me work a job. Me earn my money. Me send it home. If no be enough, what me do, me get another job. Me work hard and try to get raised up. Me open my own business, but I no pick fruit from another man tree. That's thief. What you all...you Americans like to do is plant one seed and then pick from a forest. You no plant a forest? You no around long enough for the forest to be yours. The forest no yours. You no right to pick from it. You no right. Then me state to you, you call it riddle. Or what you say is that the other man do it. Well the other man no be you. Five hundred years later you no learn that? You must know the UpCity rules are different. Who travels up here? No one. Who works here? No one.

JACQUEEDA: You work here.

CANUTE: Me struggle here. Struggle is what we do up here. Now that is what we all do. But we no always need struggle. But we struggle now. And we keep struggling if we no find a new way.

POPPY: Jah rule right?

CANUTE: Me no fi talk of Jah, for that no help. Need to find a new path. All dem religions, all them religiosity, mistake it all. Me know for true that aint but two prayers, to pass up for whoever your almighty is.

POPPY: Two prayers?

CANUTE: Only two prayers to make. All other prayers are more words than you need.

JACQUEEDA: The Lord's Prayer.

CANUTE: *(Sucks his teeth)* Ain't no father. You have a father true or no. Whether you know him or not. No lord's prayer, no act of contrition, no beneficent, no chant, aint but two prayers. When things are going according to what you anticipated—your prayer is thank you. That's all you say. When things go poorly— when your plan goes awry, and you have no idea what to do, your prayer is yes. Yes, whatever you call the name, yes. I will go with what you are sending me. I will deal with it.

JACQUEEDA: That's what they call Zen.

CANUTE: *(Sucks his teeth)* No name. No ownership. It is as it is. No nothing. Sister with her two thousand bricks, she no believe in god. Or she no call god no name. What she em do, some think foolish. What for she em do is—she em try.

POPPY: What is she doing?

CANUTE: You don't know?

JACQUEEDA: She moves bricks from one place to someplace else.

CANUTE: She no carry bricks. She no do that. She's a builder. What she does, is when she sees an empty plot of land—a land up here that is not used—she tries to build a shelter. Bricks go across in a row twenty—then she builds them up forty-one rows high. She builds it three ways round. She puts a tarp on top, to make a cover. *(Beat)* The owners? She doesn't see no owners because the land is land. Can't take it, can't own it. If nothing is on it, Sister thinks it could use a shelter. We could use a shelter. It can use a place where people can be protected from the storm.

JACQUEEDA: Not no big storm.

CANUTE: Can't nothing protect you from a big storm. A big storm, you just say, yes. They move her shelter and put nothing in its place. Prefer a lot with garbage, than a lot with shelter. She pick up her bricks and move on.

(JACQUEEDA *realizes that she is late.*)

JACQUEEDA: What time is it?

CANUTE: Time?

JACQUEEDA: They are burying my father.

CANUTE: Buried. *(Taps the shovel)*

JACQUEEDA: Buried?

CANUTE: I just finished putting the dust on the top of it.

JACQUEEDA: What do you mean?

CANUTE: Him buried at Trinity. On the left side.

JACQUEEDA: You put the dirt on him?

CANUTE: Can't wait for that type of thing. Me have other jobs to do.

JACQUEEDA: I wanted to say goodbye.

CANUTE: You wasn't saying no goodbye. The man was cold. The man was long gone. Say goodbye to someone when they can say goodbye. You wanted proof he was dead? Proof with your eyes? He was dead to you a long time.

JACQUEEDA: That man was all right.

CANUTE: The man *was* all right. Woman and man long gone. They gone. What you should do, is not moan.

Don't cry. You did not say good-bye, so live. Live your
life.

JACQUEEDA: Where am I going to place a headstone?

CANUTE: Where are you going to buy a headstone?

JACQUEEDA: The store is closed?

CANUTE: No one order head stones for Black people.

POPPY: I'm about sick of you.

CANUTE: You sick of me?

POPPY: With your smug attitude, telling people what to
do and what not?

CANUTE: I told you what I know, not what to do.

POPPY: Y'all make me sick.

CANUTE: Y'all? Who is y'all?

POPPY: Come up here taking all our stuff. Then tell us
we never had anything.

CANUTE: When did I say that? All me say is truth.
Truth, the ticket—although fraudulent—was never
yours. Her daddy, who wasn't her father anyway,
is in the ground. The Black monument store is closed.
How fe me lie?

POPPY: It's your attitude.

CANUTE: What does that do to you?

POPPY: You be talking to us like you think you better
than us.

CANUTE: Me naw for think me better than you? No
mon. Both born in the land of milk and honey.
Indoctrinated in American ways to such an extent that
all you can do is fight them. The ways American. You
have a natural disinclination toward Babylon. That is
Babylon at present, but it is the hope for the world. But

you do not attempt a solution. Me no have solution, because all for me do is work. *(He raises the shovel.)* The American Black Woman and Man has the ear of the world. The power that you have maintained by being steeled in the furnace of iniquity is what helped South Africa shed the twentieth century shackles of apartheid. Your accomplishments are admired around the world. From Angola and Algeria to Zaire and Zimbabwe. No need to look for ancient Kings and Queens in empires like Benin in past African empires. Me and African ancestors look for queens and kings on this shore.

But as I see Harlem...I come to Harlem...first day I am standing on this corner right chere. Muhammad, my brother, asks me what I see? As if my eyes see further than his. We all see the same if we can. I looked down and then I looked UpCity. He said what do you see? I said, I see what you see. Me no think, like you say, that I am better. I say, I saw, and I see that; I see it can be better. I say that they, that you, that we, can be better. It's not for me to tell a queen or a king to act, for them know. You know what you do? I don't know what a Queen or King should do, but using the second letter, spitting on the ground like the ground offended, when the ground can no offend. Letting your dogs defecate on concrete, and not picking it up. Calling everyone a nigga, or a motherfucker is not the way Queens and Kings address each other. Me no for think me better than you.

Me think you is better than you. Your nature is better than you. Me no need to instruct you on your greatness. If you don't know, ask someone who is great, cause the greatness is all around you. *(Beat)* And it is not on T V.

POPPY: Kings and Queens?

CANUTE: True both.

JACQUEEDA: Thank you.

CANUTE: No need to thank a man for tell you what you know.

POPPY: Cool.

CANUTE: And by the way—don't sit on my car.

POPPY: Your car, I thought this was the deacon's?

CANUTE: Him couldn't make the payments. I took them over. And most importantly, it aint your car.

JACQUEEDA: I thought you said I was royalty.

CANUTE: African-American royalty know correct from incorrect.

(They both get off the car.)

(They exit as the T Vs begin their glow.)

(SISTER BERRING enters empty handed.)

TWO: *I give all my power to something I don't see*

THREE: *Ultimately it is because, I want no responsibility*

FOUR: *It makes life easier for me*

FIVE: *The power is not in my hands*

TWO: *That makes it easier to be less kind*

THREE: *There but for the grace of God go I*

FOUR: *It's something you can say because you refuse to try*

TWO: *It makes you feel good*

THREE: *And there is nothing you can do*

FOUR: *For someone who is just like you*

FIVE: *Cause if you tried to help*

TWO: *God might smite you*

THREE: *It helps to give your power to someone you will never meet*

FOUR: *Because entreaties get met with enmity*

FIVE: *Since Allah told me it must be done.*

TWO: *And you must praise Jesus his only son*

THREE: *Or stop doing everything on Friday at the set of the sun.*

FOUR: *Keep the Sabbath day holy, even if you don't know when it is*

FIVE: *Saturday, Sunday, or Wednesday.*

TWO: *Keeping the power in the sky*
Makes it easier to sleep at night

THREE: *Even if you haven't tried.*

FOUR: *The future is not in heaven,*
It is in your hands

FIVE: *But to think that way*
You would have to understand

TWO: *I put my power in something I can't see*

THREE: *And I'll find fault with you if you don't believe my version of invisibility*

FOUR: *God can't make a rock that she can't move, or can she.*

FIVE: *What a question?*

TWO: *I will pray about it and leave it there.*

THREE: *My faith instead of giving me a place to grow*
Makes me stop and say that's enough.

TWO, THREE, FOUR, FIVE: *Because I believe.*

(End of Sermon)

BENEDICTION

(The day has moved on)

(The T Vs have dimmed again.)

(SISTER BERRING walks west with her two bricks.)

(CANUTE walks on.)

(They acknowledge each other.)

(CANUTE has a bunch of keys.)

(JACQUEEDA enters walking south. She has changed clothes. She is on her way to work.)

JACQUEEDA: You seen Poppy in a minute?

CANUTE: No.

JACQUEEDA: If you see him...tell him I went down to teleservices. I'll try to put him down with a job.

CANUTE: You sure him for want to work?

JACQUEEDA: He gotta work.

CANUTE: If him naw for wan work...if him just pick up a check, he may not be right there.

(She notices that he is approaching the liquor store.)

JACQUEEDA: Is that your store?

CANUTE: It no be me store. I work for the man. I don't try to get no one for go in. I just open it.

JACQUEEDA: I gotta go to work.

CANUTE: Don't we all.

(JACQUEEDA *exits. She walks south over the audience.*
CANUTE *pulls up the roll gates on the liquor store.*
The bright neon of the signs glows garishly.)

(POPPY *enters.*)

(*We see that* POPPY *has a gun in his waistband. He takes it*
out, cocks it.)

(SISTER BERRING *enters.*)

(POPPY *hides the gun.*)

(SISTER BERRING *is about to exit.*)

POPPY: Sister. Jesus...does Jesus really forgive us?

SISTER BERRING: Forgiveness? I don't think so. If you
make a mistake...well we all make mistakes...but if you
willfully act wrong, then you gotta deal with the act.
You may be forgiven, or you may not. There is no way
of knowing.

POPPY: I thought Jesus was love?

SISTER BERRING: Jesus is just a name.

POPPY: Jesus is the Lord.

SISTER BERRING: In the end was the word. And the
word was God. And the word was everyone fighting
over words. The same in the end as it was in the
beginning. Naming God. Tradition is used as a
reason not to grow. If you are wondering, if you stick
somebody up, and kill them cause your broke, or for
some other reason, will you be forgiven? Will your
conscience be cleansed? Well no. You can't go back.
Don't bet the forgiveness. If you know something is
wrong, and you know it is wrong before you do it,
don't do it.

POPPY: Leave me alone.

SISTER BERRING: You stopped me.

POPPY: I'm outta here.

SISTER BERRING: Going to work?

POPPY: Why does everyone ask me that?

SISTER BERRING: If you aint going to work what are you doing?

POPPY: Sight seeing.

(She laughs)

SISTER BERRING: What sights you get to see up here?

POPPY: A lot of madness.

SISTER BERRING: Madness.
  Sight seeing. Up here the sights to see. People go out and try to count the white people.

POPPY: White people do that too.

SISTER BERRING: Sure it's a sight to see. They would count Black people, but that would be too hard up here.

POPPY: What you doing?

SISTER BERRING: I got something to do.

(She looks at him, and then exits.)

(CANUTE enters.)

POPPY: You wanna buy a gun?

CANUTE: I don't need a gun.

POPPY: For protection?

CANUTE: I don't need no protection. Sell it downtown.

POPPY: I don't need any police in my life.

CANUTE: Go to Brooklyn with it then.

POPPY: Too far.

CANUTE: The Bronx.

POPPY: Like, it'll never find its way back over the bridge.

CANUTE: Who'd you get it from?

POPPY: Someone. He won't take it back. Doesn't know where it's been.

(POPPY *uncocks the pistol*)

(*Puts it back in his waistband.*)

(*The televisions begin to glow again.*)

(*The T Vs show a series of religious symbols. The audience only sees the glow of them.*)

(SISTER BERRING *comes on stage.*)

SISTER BERRING: *If you want to prove*
That you love God
Take care, of each other
Take care, of each other
Cause when you get down to it
That is all we've got.

(*A T V falls out of a window and smashes on the concrete.*)

(SISTER BERRING *looks at the fallen T V. She walks off.*)

(*The song continues.*)

(CANUTE *brings out the broom and dustpan, and cleans the T V.*)

(*Liquor store signs grow bright.*)

END OF PLAY

www.ingramcontent.com/pod-product-compliance
Lightning Source LLC
Chambersburg PA
CBHW070030110426

42741CB00035B/2712